Talking to Stanley on the Telephone

Also by Michael Schmidt

Poetry

Very Selected, Smith|Doorstop, 2017
Selected Poems, Smith|Doorstop, 2014
The Stories of My Life, Smith|Doorstop, 2013
New and Collected Poems, Sheep Meadow, 2010
Collected Poems, Smith|Doorstop, 2009
The Resurrection of the Body, Smith|Doorstop 2006, Sheep Meadow, 2007
The Love of Strangers, Century Hutchinson, 1989
Choosing a Guest: new and selected poems, Anvil, 1983

Anthologies

New Poetries I–VIII, Carcanet, 1994–2021
The Great Modern Poets, Quercus, 2006
The Harvill Book of Twentieth-Century Poetry in English, Harvill, 1999

Talking to Stanley on the Telephone

Michael Schmidt

smith|doorstop

the poetry business

Published 2021 by The Poetry Business
Campo House,
54 Campo Lane,
Sheffield S1 2EG
www.poetrybusiness.co.uk

Copyright © Michael Schmidt 2021
The moral rights of the author have been asserted.
ISBN 978-1-912196-44-9

All rights reserved.
Without limiting the rights under copyright reserved above,
no part of this publication may be reproduced, storied in or introduced
into a retrieval system, or transmitted, in any form or by any means
(electronic, mechanical, photocopying, recording or otherwise),
without the prior written permission of both the copyright owner
and the above publisher of this book.

Designed & typeset by The Poetry Business.
Printed by Imprint Digital
Cover Painting: *Western Electric Rotary Phone & Blue Table*
by Christopher Stott (https://christopher-stott.tumblr.com/)

Acknowledgement and thanks are due to Herb Leibowitz, editor of *Parnassus*,
and to Ann and Peter Sansom, editors of *The North*, where 'About Homer'
first appeared.

British Library Cataloguing-in-Publication Data.
A catalogue record for this book is available from the British Library.

Smith|Doorstop is a member of Inpress
www.inpressbooks.co.uk.
Distributed by NBN International, 1 Deltic Avenue,
Rooksley, Milton Keynes MK13 8LD.

The Poetry Business gratefully acknowledges the support
of Arts Council England.

Poems written in age confuse the years.
We all live, said Bashō, in a phantom dwelling.
Judith Wright, 'The Shadows of Fire: Ghazals'

For Miles Burrows

Contents

Before

- 11 Exceptions
- 13 First and Last Things
- 14 Running Away
- 16 Anniversary
- 17 Guo Nian
- 18 The Costume Party
- 19 *Alone with the Hairy Ainu; Or, 3800 Miles on a Pack Saddle in Yezo and a Cruise to the Kurile Islands* by A. H. Savage Landor (1893)
- 21 Walkie Talkie
- 23 A Bright Jewel in an Aethiope's Ear
- 26 The Lord of Aratta
- 27 Chaque cheveu a sa place
- 29 Mercy
- 31 Saint Thomas's

After

- 35 The Bath
- 36 Hair and Memory
- 37 Saying *Thank You*
- 38 Threes
- 40 To the Dentist
- 41 Tuba Mirum
- 44 Sunday Morning
- 48 An Easter Carol for Edward Taylor
- 51 Stanley and Me
- 52 Bedside Table
- 54 Annunciation
- 56 About Homer: an epyllion

BEFORE

Exceptions

Texas, 1950

Yes, I could read.
             *No dogs
or Mexicans* the large
round caps declared. 'Papa,
we can't go in.' My new
red passport said as much.
'They don't mean us.' He pushed
open the loud screen door
to a stale interior.

Little white serviettes
defined the seating plan.
Ketchup, French mustard. Our
bug-spattered Pontiac
with dust-dulled number plates
said 'Mexico D.F.'
It shivered in the heat.

He was right. They didn't
mean us. We fit, our skin
at home. The slow-bladed
ceiling fan made shadows
surge and plunge, like breathing.
They served us up the stuff
they'd eat themselves, unspiced,
prepared for the littlest
bear, neither too salty
nor sweet, not too hot or
too cold. We sipped, we smeared
bland red and yellow on
our burgers, overdone;

and grinning there, alert,
infernal black and brown,
a monster Doberman.

First and Last Things

There was, first off, the house we seemed to build
    Up in a tree, or under the floor, and lived
With all our creatures and with all we were –
    Pirate and doctor, sailor, angel, priest;
And then the first house made of mud or brick
    Furnished with whatever we could find
Of real stuff, like wood and parakeets
    And cushions, pottery and even framed
Pictures on the walls, they were real walls,
    Nails could be driven into them.
The pictures were of us as we grew older
    And they faded with us too as we grew older
The way pictures do or antique mirrors
    Discolour as the isinglass gets tired
Of showing what is there and turns instead
    Interpreter, an eschatologist
Who shows only what will be, which in the longer term
    Is, after all, what is, and ever shall be.

Running Away

When they called I was running away, from the first call, running.
As soon as I could, I ran. Before, I'd imagined running
Away from the liquor amnii, the rippling endometrium,
The muscles' hum and squeeze, light breaking into the hot
    cramped cave,
Tugging the cord until it gave way, I was running away
From the snare, from the needle, the prick in the heel,
    the swaddling,
The sweet acrid smell of her skin (the slime and talcum were mine),
From the breast, the shiny spoon, the tub and the tepid water,
Apple scent that was soapy and made grey froth on the water,
The light that hurt the eyes and the dark that was so like water.
As I ran I shouted and hollered. I floated on tears.
I gave them no peace. They'd waked me up, no sleep for them.
Had I known, as soon as that half cell of me flushed from his body
Entering the throbbing shaft of her I'd have chosen a way
To not be. But I was, without a choice in the matter except
Running away.   I ran when they called, I took my bandana
And a long stick and packed some cookies and Coke for the
    journey.
I would go where the stories led (at night they read me stories).
I walked down the long porch to the gate and was crying. *Goodbye*,
She said, *and don't be late for supper*. At the back of the house
In the new orchard I sat and waited for them to follow
To force me back the way they always did. I sat and the stars
Started up. When would they come? They did not come. They'd
    forgotten.
It was dinner time, they started without me.
    When I returned,
My face was streaked with a different flavour of tears. *You're late*,
He said but not angry. They'd taken my measure, it was time

To run away in different directions, on subtler feet
So long as they followed, they had to follow, panting,
They had to follow, calling, calling, growing older,
Growing weaker, they had to follow as a moth follows candlelight
And then just before they touched the flame they had to
Alter their wing beat, turn off their hearts, drop into dark.

Anniversary

When I am sleeping things occur. You come
Back from the dead, I lift the big stone off you,
It weighs no more than a feather, you stand
And stretch and look, though not at me because
I am asleep. You walk right through me.
You leave prints in the dirt and your shadow
Moves close beside you, shadow cast by moonlight,
As though an intimate has come back with you
Holding your hand, sharing your pulse and posture.
You have upon you the smell of mildew and soil
And that sweetness you always wore is palpable and yes,
You walk right through me and I feel your heart again
Pummelling the bone bars inside your chest
And in your throat and lungs the rasping that killed you
Not the phlegmy prelude to your funeral,
More now like a hoarse hymn of resurrection.
Down at the cemetery gate you linger,
Step out into the road with its yellow lamps,
Look, your shadow also, towards town, then uphill.
No one familiar. No one, not even a car.
You turn and come back in, and go back home
To the place we put you, marked, and in time forgot,
Walking right through me you find the spot
Among the pine shrubs, by the wind-shaped oak,
Lie down again and pull the soil tight up
Under your chin, and close your hazel eyes.
The big stone weighs too much for me, your shadow
Helps me replace it. Daylight comes in.

Guo Nian

Shānyáng? Miányáng?
for Eddie Hsu

Is it the year of the sheep, the goat, the antelope?
I'm confused, and you who should know because
It is your calendar, and language is your subject,
Say with a smile, *It's a problem of translation*,
And that's the end of it! But I want to know
Is it the year of the billy, buck, hogget or ram,
The nanny, the wether, the kid, the silver chevron?
Of blubbery mutton? Or is it the year of the lamb?

It is the year of the lamb, the first soft creature
Man brought home and tended and gathered for grazing
On a hill, down shadowy valleys, to the plain,
Reared for its wool, for its music, for its sweet beard,
Herded and drove to the fold, kept from the wolf
And tended and slept among at Choga Mami
In Diyarbakir, in Jericho and here in Doggerland.

It's the year of the lamb, the first soft creature
We took to our hearths and hearts and tended, we cared for,
The first creature we reared for coarse cloth and cheeses,
For trust, the merry bleating in upland pastures
And in April, bruised salvia, sage, dew-drenched, at sunrise
We dress it, cense the altar, whetting a paschal razor,
Blood on our wrists, in our gullets, the steaming oblation
That blesses us still as we slit its quavering throat.

The Costume Party

How, without a by your leave, can we decently go?
The annoying dog with his wet nose up your skirt,
The meagre canapes, the piddling cocktails ...
But much may yet occur. And then, perhaps
If we go we won't be missed at all!
But missed is what we want to be.
Why come all this way, in costumes, too,
And not have them declare
                        Stay on a while,
It gets better and better, or, *Why,*
Nothing much has happened yet, don't leave! or
You're the very life and soul, without a witch,
Without a moose the fun will all be over!
                                       We'll feel
They wanted us to stay if they say that
And, going, leave a little sort of disappointment,
Get home content in time for the soaps and supper.

What if they don't? We say *We have to leave you*
And they reply *OK, mind how you go*
And we just go, what then? No broken heart,
Regret, not even *We've not had time for a proper visit!*
Not yet! We might as well
Not have come at all, we'll get
No party bag, all we'll have to take home
On the slow rush hour bus, apart from your
Broomstick and my bobbing rubber antlers
Is hair from the nosey dog that begged us to stroke it,
Mouse-grey hair from that dog, its smell on our hands,
The dog that didn't even bite us, a hair of him.

Alone with the Hairy Ainu; Or, 3800 Miles on a Pack Saddle in Yezo and a Cruise to the Kurile Islands by A. H. Savage Landor (1893)

I was reading *Alone with the Hairy Ainu*.
It was the only book in the house.
Light was fading, the house was cold,
The smell of cooking from next door
Said fish and cabbage, fish and cabbage.
Even fish and cabbage would have been nice.
    I had never been to Japan, and to my knowledge
Had never met or even seen an Ainu.
The descriptions made them feel warm,
Like stuffed animals or rugs or fur coats.
It was so cold I almost forgot that they are people
And imagined wrapping myself in one,
Or pressing myself between two and getting warm
Like a toasted cheese and ham panini.
Then as night came on and the pages
Disappeared in shadow I kept saying to myself
You are among them, they're your friends,
They're your fuel, they're your illumination.
If you get much hungrier you may have to eat one.
    I went to sleep and when I woke up it was dark.
There were no Ainu and I was alone
In the ice-cold house with only the one book,
No light, no duvet, no food.
(I could have eaten even cabbage, even fish,
But next door had had its dinner, washed its plates,
The only smells were ice and snow and drains.)
I felt a longing so intense for the hairy Ainu,

Aunt or mother, sister Ainu, niece,
I would have married one or all of them,
I would have hugged them. I was so in love
Not for the first time. And they weren't at home.

Walkie Talkie

for *Neil Astley and Pamela Robertson-Pearce*

I am at the airport. Gulls take off and are landing.
It is terminal three. I started at terminal one
In error, and sprinted along the moving walkways
Dragging my wheelie bag with its plaintive wheel,
Scattering small change and apologies.
Now my plane is late. And now my plane is cancelled.
I spend a euro and sit on an Alibaba
Airport Massage Chair and jitter to calm my nerves.
It doesn't last very long. I get up unsteadily
And stand still for a moment thinking what and why,
Then I give in to the music and the pulsing lights,
I walk from outlet to outlet, I buy from a huge rack
An inflatable striped neck halter, red and yellow, which I blow up,
Then at the duty free I spray Hugo Boss Intense,
Hugo Boss Motion, Night, Orange, Man of Today,
Eau de Toilette, Scent for Him, Energise, Just Different, Iced
On my left wrist with my right hand, on my right wrist with my
        left.
I can't get the smells off by rubbing with spit on a tissue:
I stand like a queasy lamp-post ten civet cats have visited
The steaming contents of their perineal glands on,
Then go to the Gents and scrub with scentless soap.
In Electronix I try the headsets, Sony, Beats, Bose, Euasoo
I settle on the yellow and black Binatone Walkie Talkie
(Discounted), two handsets, with a three km range,
Then return to the massage chair to adjust my purchases,
Take off my backpack, gather it into my lap
As if it were a child I wanted to stay asleep.
I put on my halter and spend another euro. We two,
Backpack and I, sit together vibrating for the precisely
Three minutes our money buys, after which I settle

Into the not quite soft upholstery. Like a stone
I begin to sink away from rainbow neons into dozing
Turquoise sea light, down and down in tepid dark
Without coming to rest, down, down, a flat
Stone that does not plummet but rocks right left, right left,
As if like a seed it had some intelligence beyond physics
And knew what it was doing, how it almost danced
Except it was alone and sank keeping time
Into time, going deeper, deeper, finding no seabed.

A Bright Jewel in an Aethiope's Ear

for John McAuliffe

That was Stockport. No one got off at Stockport.
It's after midnight. Very nearly home.
Are you awake still? I was saying,
Tone is part of content: for instance,
He's a person of integrity is one thing,
He's a person of 'integrity' quite another.
A grimace is not a smile
Though it draws with the same twenty-six muscles.
Integrity, 'integrity', suspend
Those earrings on each side of the word,
      its face is altered.
Beauty means beauty, but *'beauty'*?
Every fissure in the makeup surfaces,
Parched map, parchment, it doesn't matter
If the earrings are dangly with seed pearls
Or hammered tin and sharp-edged glass.

    It's dark out there:
Longsight, still as doom, or is that Heaton Chapel ...
The train slows, stalls. It coughs and goes to sleep.
Are you awake?
    Imagine being home already with
Your shrill Chihuahua, calmed after Harrington's
Turkey and Veg and her Dental Daily. You're prone
On the giant canvas bean-bag watching telly,
She's sound asleep above your stomach,
Curled up warm (so small)
With trust and custom on your sternum.
    Imagine being at the office. It's tomorrow,
You've got your Danish and skinny latte from Prêt,
You chew crisp cinnamon and sip, stand at the floor

To ceiling window gazing at the crane-littered city,
Its erratic ups and downs, a crazy dazzle and
Some huge black and white clouds piled
Steep behind it with their rather more
Short-term, stormy version of the future.
(The boss is off in Dublin, no one's watching.)

      What's the littlest thing
      You can spin a poem out of,
What half-memory, blip or echo, mote?
The stillness of the train wedged in darkness,
A night-stifled suburb whose streets
Only vermin circulate, tired corpuscles
Carrying, carrying on, rats and mice, marking
B-roads for return to holes and burrows;
Foxes, jaded and ravenous, overturn bins,
Burst bags and scrabble, brushes tucked away;
Gaping, agog, citizens wheeze and snore,
Chugging darkness after making
Or thinking they've made careful love,
Dreaming of worlds they're saving up for, or will buy
When the postcode lottery knocks at the door.
      And the homeless
Wait patient for us at Piccadilly Station
With paper cups and bulldogs, we're the last providers
Before they too turn in under the bridges.

My Fitbit's almost out of battery.
My phone is dead already and besides
It's too late to ring anyone but Stanley
And I have absolutely nothing to say to him.
The train sighs and considers
Is it time to move? It's time to move.
      It does not move.
Are you awake still? I was saying

Tone is part of content. At this hour
And in this place, stuck on the rails like rust,
Tone is part of content, part of content.

The Lord of Aratta

I've received too many acronyms for one day.
LOLs and SOZs, DOLs and KO and ME2 and PSH
Were bad enough, but then the emojis started
And are far worse. Two dozen smileys have come in
This morning, each differently inclined, inflected,
Cats and donkeys and what may be bondage handcuffs,
Stylised bits of humans, syringe, a safety-pin,
A rifle, spider and a rocket ship, mushroom
Or a mushroom cloud. A cactus.
                                    I know
How the Lord of Aratta felt when he received
From Babylon the first sun-baked clay tablet sent
From great King Enmerkar proposing terms for peace
Or for surrender, and since he couldn't make out
The wedgy shapes' sense, much less their sounds, he narrowed
His eyes and stared and stared and while he was staring
His army killed time. He gawked at the message
While Enmerkar's sly soldiers climbed the walls and placed
A noose around his bent neck and hung him, as still
He squinted at the muddy tablet in his palm
And couldn't extrude the spell, or how to spell it.

Chaque cheveu a sa place

Being a barber, what I see is hair
And partings, angled, straight; a cowlick; curls
Spring from the comb, teasing the scissor's bite.

I see the scalp and sometimes flecks of skin
Litter the furrows the comb's teeth draw straight –
Snowflakes in fields, where pheasants dip and drink.

I have the bright shampoos in stoppered phials
And unguents, powders, pomades, puffs, balms, oils.
I have the looking glass that in reverse

Displays the evidence of what I've done
As an echo confirms what I declare
Or *amen* makes a prayer (with grace) come true.

I like the balding best. I feel the bone.
The baldness is a test, the purest thing
A barber has to deal with. It's the truth.

Down is fine, tiny, too short for clippers.
I unfold and strop the straight-edge razor,
Try it with my thumb. I fill the bristles

Of the round-headed badger brush with foam.
I froth the scalp and rake the blade right over,
Wiping it clean on my white steaming cloth.

I towel the pate dry as you might restore
A baby. When I'm done I hand it back
Polished smooth as agate, scented, entire,
The ears still in place, the puckered forehead,

Chaque cheveu a sa place ... or, rather, each
Surface as it should be, as it will be

Thoughtless, memoryless. You hold it in both
Hands gingerly and sniff, tip it this way,
That way, say *So*, lift it on. It fits still.

I powder your neck, sweep the collar clear,
Unpin and fold away the checked chair cloth.
The girl at the exit smiles. The door chimes.

The boy who's learning sweeps the nothing up.

Mercy

She is not dead, but sleeping.
                        No, she's dead.
I visited just before, just after.
I saw her in the box with her black dress on,
Shoes shinier than they'd ever been in Cross Street,
Face fixed in a rouged grimace, mortician work.
I watched them screw the top on, on the day
Helped carry her to church and set her down
On wobbly trestles. With the others
I withdrew, knelt and said the words while she
Stayed dead. At the Amen
We shouldered her once more,
Climbed to a graveyard full of dark birds drawn
To the rectangle dug in winter soil
There by the yew, and lined with AstroTurf,
The only green in February.
We inched her down and down
On those wide beige ribbons made of what feels like leather.
Our gloves stuck to our hands, each one of us
Struggling in his breath cloud, ice on our cheeks.
Her widower threw the first handful of earth
Tenderly. Her daughter Gertrude and her son,
Bundled up so I couldn't read their faces,
Each tossed soil on the coffin lid with a sound of sizzling
Then one by one we came with our raised fists,
Threw, wiped our hands clean on handkerchiefs.
After, the sexton finished it off with shovels full
And tamped, the birds waiting for us to go
So they could peck grubs live out of loosened soil.
Were she not dead but sleeping
Think how it would be when she woke up,
Reached for specs, water-glass, rosary,

Moving her leg out from the shroud
Groping for a slipper. Where's the light switch?
Just tight ceiling, wall and wall and wall, no room.
Now she'd be waking up, gasping for light
She'd be living out the darkest dream of all,
That after the cuts and bruises last year,
Buckets of her own offal, bone and excrement,
Weeks of sores, daily diminution,
Tubes, the chemo, pain re-emerging
From under morphine's clement veil,
Laying hold – not over – this is the ever after.
Better cut in stone the kinder truth –
She is not sleeping, she is dead and buried.

Saint Thomas's

He's getting married. I've been there, I've been married
In a much bigger church than this one, but emptier,
With fewer flowers. I don't remember any flowers.
I did not have bridesmaids or pageboys, either,
No crimson sashes, buttonholes, at the door
No mournful bagpipe, kilts, a long black limo.
The petals – I didn't have petals strewn up the aisle to the altar,
Or a printed order of service with portraits, his and hers.
In my congregation I recall twelve restless acquaintances,
One in-law in yellow, an edgy fat priest. Was there music?
The memory is entirely devoid of sound.
Saint Thomas's on the other hand while we wait has music.
It makes you think my neighbour whispers
Without saying just what it makes you think about.
Worse than think, it makes you remember, I want to reply.
– He's getting married to her, despite what he knows
Of all she's been up to, and it's hard not to laugh, but she'll be
Swathed in white like butter never melted,
And a veil that he'll draw back like bedroom curtains
After a night of love in the dark and there she'll be.
What will she look like at that moment when she's it,
Forsaking all other, until death (for the time being).
– He's not much better. She knows about that I suppose,
Half the men here waiting for her big entrance
On her lap of honour up the rosy nave
Know him as she never will, myself among them.
The blocks we've been around! A city of them. He stands there
In black awaiting white, like ink patient for paper,
Like night (all those nights!) who knows his day will come
Though he's put it off and off successfully until now.
    The organ swells, she emerges, with papa to whose elbow
She adheres, a sail fixed to a stocky mast,

A spinnaker, say. She billows, navigating with effort
Because of the train, the impossible heels and the child
In utero a little longer. The father,
Looking surprised, is sweating, he sort of struts beside her.
They arrive at the first pew where the mother
Is dabbing her eyes and lips and averts her gaze.
The groom steps away from his shadow to receive her.
Attached, they turn as instructed to the priest.
He welcomes them, and there is God behind him,
And behind God the tunnel of the future,
And behind that all the pasts in a tangle, debris
Of accidents that happen time after time.
No one admits to *any just let or hindrance*.
They declare their vows with a memorised inflection
And are proclaimed. *You may kiss the bride*, the priest says
(Not *you may kiss the groom*?) and we applaud
As at a performance when the curtain's falling
And we are released to go out into rain
And make our own way five blocks to the reception
In the Olympia Ball Room, to await the limo
And there'll be speeches, back-slapping, the new couple
Will lead out the first dance, and eventually the guests
Will melt away into the rain. It's always raining
Unless it's snowing. I've been there. I've been married.

AFTER

The Bath

Sometimes, but much less often than before,
My heart-faced penis rises in the bath,
Breaking the surface with unplanned desire.
We nod at one another, then we gaze.
We're not at home as we once were. He has
Nothing fresh to say, and nor do I.
He regains self-possession, retracts and is gone.
That's it. I'm disappointed. I go after,
But even a good scrub will not revive
What old age and malignancy unstrung.
I get out and wrap myself in a huge blue towel.
It was not always thus or often thus.
I'm grateful all the same that, now and then,
He comes back unbidden in case we have
Some business to transact, old rumour, love.

Hair and Memory

On the bed she has turned to clay and her bare feet
Have become clay and her long-fingered hands
Are clay. Also her mouth and lips and the not quite sealed
Sliver of eye and her hair and memory, clay.
Her love is clay. Her lover is clay like her.
I am clay like her. I am like her. I am clay.

Saying Thank you

On sixteen legs they walk you up the aisle.
We say some things, we weep a little bit.
We sing a hymn you chose – why did you choose
That silly hymn of all the silly hymns
In *Hymns for Today*?

On sixteen legs they bear you down the aisle,
Out through the Great Door into too hot sunlight.
In what you liked to call *the Black Maria* they ferry you
To where you are reduced to ash and canned.
They hand the can to me and I say *Thank you*.
I have you. I fold my handkerchief away.

Threes

They've took his kidney out, and look at him,
The porter says, shunting him into his bay.
Bet he's wanting to go home.
                               I bet he isn't.
He looks as though they've took his kidney out,
Poor chap, pale as butter, eye-whites a dark shade of piss
When, groaning, gargling, he comes round.
He grins, grimaces, and though I haven't asked,
Calls across the aisle to tell me about the operation.
The kidney was *this big*, he can show me a picture
(The surgeon sent it on after sewing him up).
Later, I say, and swallow, and have to listen.
Then his wife arrives, his daughter, they draw the curtain.
In private he tells them the same story
In the same loud voice, as though it was a folk tale,
Same words, *this big*, and he shows them the photo
Because they squeal in disbelief and revulsion.

I have nothing to show for my stay here,
No organ uprooted, no wound, no carved scar.
The catheter balloon has been deflated
(I thought it was filled with air, but no, they use saline)
And the whole mess of it pulled out of my urethra
And dropped in a red bucket. *If you can pee
Three times – here are the three containers, numbered –*
The cheerful nurse declares, *you can go home.*
The threes are out of fairy tales, the imprisoned prince
Must overcome these challenges; the containers
Are shaped like boots you'd put on a large dog
Or a golf club, a driver or three wood, say. Of course
I cannot pee, not one exiguous drop.
I sit and think about peeing.

I drink jug after jug of water without result
Apart from a tiny jet of fire which the cheerful nurse
Says is insufficient, I must start again.
                              I think of rivers,
I think of water roaring between steep cliff walls,
The boat outrunning the current, fast as a plane.
Of *Euphrates, Araxes and similar rivers* ...
In my frumpish hospital gown I dream I'm soaring
Into a cumulus and coming down
As a patter of rain (call it rain) on Danae's umbrella.
I think of waterfalls, lagoons, warm lakes;
Of saunas, tubs, jacuzzis; of beer and cider.
I ask for more tea, more coffee. I ask for milk.
I play the bed controls, fold myself up, unfold myself;
I watch TV, I drink another pitcher.
The man without a kidney falls asleep.
His wife and daughter tiptoe out, going back
Grateful, briskly, as if almost out of patience,
Into their own lives. I lift again the first container
And point my bewildered penis into its dark.

To the Dentist

The third time the crown fell off and I had to go back,
In the waiting room there was a new *Hello* to wait with.
On this occasion the amalgam had come loose
In a piece of fruit cake and I swallowed it. Next day
It signalled to me from the toilet pan as if it was
A thumbnail of silver escaping a lump of ore.
Prospector, I gingerly prised it out,
Broke it free, rinsed it off, and let it
Soak all day in a mug of Listerine.

I read *Hello*, it was the Megan's pregnant number,
And wondered whether my dentist, Mr Osman Lebatt,
Would like to know how the crown had been retrieved
Or would he prefer once again to restore it, batten it down,
Without the back story, with his usual parting injunction
To *mind how you go* after all his thick rubber fingers
Had enlarged my mouth, tugging, pushing, packing down,
Leaving the crown again too high, so the mouth can't quite close,
Like a verse with rather too many syllables jockeying for position in
    the final line.

Tuba Mirum

I never liked him much. He smiled a lot.
Even when we were twelve
He was always having to go 'off to rehearsals'.
He was overweight, and unctuous, and successful.
Yet though I never liked him,
Time after time I accepted his invitations.
Even now. And we never lost touch
The way I've lost touch with my real mates year by year,
With Oli, Dominic, Lorenzo, Malachi,
With Hammad, Avery, and worst of all, Xavier.
There's only him left now of all of them.

Tonight, he told me, *is a big one for me*.
Not only Mussorgsky's 'Bald Mountain'
(Which makes him chuckle ever since I've gone bald)
And part of Vaughan Williams's hideous 'Concerto
For Tuba'; he wants me also to meet *her*,
He wants her to meet his *oldest friend*.

I settle back, third row stalls (he knows where I'm sitting).
The lights begin to dim, then a spot picks him out.
He shuffles on stage in tails with his enormous horn,
Spaghetti Junction condensed in brass
Under an ample arm. The giant bell reflects
          Dozens of upturned faces;
Fading bulbs of the great chandelier
Multiply in it, set free like swarms of fire-flies.
They make their own applause, laughter of light
Glinting off jewels, bling, teeth and glasses.
He bows, the tuba bows, the orchestra
Tenses, takes a breath; fat lips adjust,
He emits a sonorous kiss and they're all off,

Elbows pumping like a flock of geese
           Struggling to get airborne.

Quite soon the effort mesmerises,
Ears muffle the noise, music turns
To the cacophony one's used to in traffic,
The taxi radio plays something almost familiar,
Horns, brakes and wipers follow their own sound route,
An ambulance, then a fire truck's woo-woo woo-woo
Like lines on a post-modern score that flare, collide and cross.
It's sleepy when the fireflies are extinguished.

I never liked him much, though he liked me.
He used to find me by the pond and bring me cake
His mother'd baked, and later pills and weed.
After a while I went to his school parades.
He wore a gilded red-and-blue uniform,
Hugged his eighteen knotted feet of horn
Tight as he stepped and puffed and sweated
Marching alone in his back row because he was big.
One time in a cold rehearsal room he made me
Hold the huge instrument and press my lips to the mouthpiece
Still damp from his music and tasting of mint pastilles
And blow a noise into it. He tried to show me
How the stops worked, pressing my fingers down with his,
Leaning kiss-close and wheezing.
                                    That girl on the second double bass
With the crimson frock and the generous cleavage he'd described
Must be his Albanian inamorata, Ajkuna.
She wears black lipstick, plays doggedly, eyes riveted on him
As if he is already legally hers.
I try not to imagine them together, but there they are,
The huge horn with its sensuous volutions,
The double base gulping sound like a hollow tree,
Those mouths, those elbows, armpits, sweat and spit.

When it's over, applause, the audience
Filtering into the dark, I wait for him.
He comes without his horn, and on his elbow
Draws her without her double bass close after.
I think I know what is required. He smiles
Dimples in his dimples; she holds on.
Music's not really my thing, I remark.
              I come for old time's sake.
She might have said *I know, I heard you snoring*
But likes the thought that he might have a 'best man'.
That's his big question, which he springs, and I can't say no.
The date has not been set, but in the next
Six months or so. They'll devise their own vows
And make their music, too, a stout duet.
We go to a pub nearby for Prosecco and peanuts.
Then I congratulate and loosely hug the lucky couple
And leave them.
         Outside,
There are no taxis to be had, which is just as well.
Best man means a new suit and formal shoes.
It means a stag night and a speech. I never
Liked him much. I don't like her. I don't like
'Till Eulenspiegel' or 'Petroushka', either,
Though I have sat through both because he asked me.
I take the late tube and then an empty bus to Becontree.
Low mist hangs all across Dagenham, a rural feel
Of Essex, I like to call it Essex. It really was
Before the giant factories started, then stopped.
Midnight cool and mist put a memory
Of grass and clover back under my feet.
There are almost barns and pastures, cattle
Snoring in enclosures ...
            Then, the junction.
The zebra crossing. Stuttering neons. Blinding LEDs.
A late lorry snarls through its ten gears.

Sunday Morning

for Herb Leibowitz at 85

It's Sunday. I think *church*. I plump the pillow
As if to pump the organ up with music.
I roll onto my stomach, subside, select
Out of the stale, sweet air of completed sleep,
A processional, fill the airy softness
With gruff enchantment, adoration, tried verse.

When did I last attend church? The seductive
Vicar, smiling, red-cheeked, like the unnamed fruit
That tempted Eve, asks me whenever we meet
In the street, graveyard or the aisles of Lidl's,
Can we welcome you next Sunday? And I say
By all means, vicar, and I mean it, the smile
Is worth eliciting, libidinal grace.
 (The sunny graveyard exhaled fresh camomile
Where we paused: you brushed the bush with your sandals.)

What did I want to say when you distracted
Me with your lilt, you charming servant of God?
This is what I ought to have thought of saying.
I don't come nowadays: something's gone awry.
Not music, there's always that, not harmonies,
Not a speaker with a halo or a sword,
Not words but the warp and woof that conjure up
The palpable Word, that turn sound into prayer
And memory (prayer that binds times together,
Last week and this, this old age and that childhood –
I remember I remembered this before –),
And what was congregation, whatever we
Might think of galling neighbours back in clock time,
Offset by speaking the same words together,

Inherited, unarguable patterns
With measure answering the call of sense, the call
Of all the senses registered: in the thighs,
Belly, the heart and head, and all the members
Answering that call as if one body. Putting
Words together as we are intended to,
They possess volume in both senses, they weigh
With gravity, they sound, have tone like colour.
They're made and they are making, praise and conjure,
Snare and bring down, unhurt, Dominions, Angels,
Out of the air, the spirit, and they listen,
Respond, they kneel and touch. Heaven's no closer
But its people are.
                    You might have understood –
But your red mobile would have detonated,
'A parishioner in need!' and off you'd go
To someone's last goodbye with your phial of oils.
When a sacrament begins you put on wings
To soar and dive, to raise up and then bring down
The grace entrusted to you. You are transformed
To the soutane, black robes. Vocation takes you.
I bet when you start to fly your shoulders hurt.

We're no longer one to one when I attend
St Audrey's in New Town. You belong to all
Equally. I cross the threshold and look up
The archaic nave: there's starved Jesus, leaning
Out of the shadows, ribs sharp as a bar code,
His bloody hands make two helpless heart-shaped fists
Around the spikes. What comfort's He for people
Whose nerves emit a red jet of warning pain
That says, *Be getting ready, night is falling*.
The abscess is preparing, the kidney stone,
The broken rib, the break just above the heart.

Out on my loggia an obese red robin,
Stops to take a look in. I look back at him,
My stunted apple tree, my potted orange,
The straggling herbs, especially the fennel
Splayed by wind and rain in a feathery star.
Ailanthus leaves rebound in the drizzle.

I lie on my back, intuiting the pulse
The rain gives to the leaves, and the fat robin
Chirrups as if to start a conversation.
It's Sunday, says the bird. I plump the pillow
As if to pump the organ up with music.

An Easter carol took form in his throat ...

An Easter Carol for Edward Taylor

in memory of Michael Powell

Long fields of yellow wheat
In Palestinian sun
Are ripening into flesh.
The vineyards on the hill
Bring forth a salty fruit.

There where the bread was torn
Off of the human loaf,
Where years began to count
Because a child was born
I come to eat my Word.

Before me at the rail
Is Stephen with the stones
Turned into loaves by love
And James of Zebedee
Carries his singing head;

Peter and Philip bear
Splinters of their cross trees,
Bartholomew his skin
Rolled up beneath his arm,
Thomas from India

With his appalling spear,
And sweet Sebastian too,
God's willing porcupine,
And Agatha whose heart
Is caroling with hurt,
Perpetua with her own new
Baby clutched at her breast,

Felicity her slave
Whose child will not be born
Attended by the beasts

That tore them limb from limb
And slouch now tame and meek
To Bethlehem, and kneel
The way the sheep and ox
Knelt on that first day.

Cyprian and Polycarp
Both try to sneak away
But drawn by the infant Host
Out-dazzling from his crib
The flare of martyrs' fires

(Antipas on the grill –
Domitian's brazen bull,
And all the melting saints
That lit his jubilees,
And later La Pucelle,

And in a northern town
Cranmer and Ridley too,
Transcendent kindling,
Making the tongues of flame
Speak so we understood)
They climb their Calvary
Carrying such precious gifts
As Africa can spare.
There where the wine was spilled
Out of the Virgin's womb

Belief and disbelief,
Faithful and faithless, kneel

Because, whatever's true,
A child is going to grow
On whom we can impress

Fear, hatred and desire,
A child we will impale
And plant in every grave.
We do it by the Book.
I come to eat my Word.

Stanley and Me

for Stanley Moss

Stanley's got the big poems up his sleeve:
Love and life and death, and all those landscapes,
The rivers of the world and every mountain

He's sat at the foot of, or climbed to the top of,
Meditating sage-like, tree-like, stone-like,
Or making love to yet another dazzling dryad.

I'm old. Though he's a good deal older,
Accelerating towards exit velocity,
He keeps the steering stick firmly in his hand

Defying, an inch below the exosphere,
God's most officious angels: they grab at him,
He hurtles by, they just can't get a handle.

Stanley's got the big poems, and he leaves to me,
Exhausted, wasted, rueful, out of breath
Even on the stairs to the loft, not much –

Things he overlooked. How little
Can I make my poem out of? That scrap, this
Almost nothing? On the plate: where his

Pork chop steamed, gnawed bone now, a gravy
Ideogram and – that at least's entirely mine –
A bright blob of Colman's ablaze at the lip.

Bedside Table

I put my specs on an open book under the lamp
On the bedside table, and they start to read.
       They gather pace, they skim,
Turning the pages somehow, fast as fingers.

I remove and set my dentures on a plate by the book.
They start pronouncing words, the words the specs read.
My false teeth and my spectacles ... I am
Attentive as a child, they're telling a story.
If I'd put new batteries in my hearing aids
I might have followed. As it is: just crackling.

Maybe the story's one where I still have hair,
I am rather young, I have a lover who's young,
Darker than I am, smaller, stronger, too,
Talking my first language with a cheeky accent,
Then picking up a book (not one I've written)
And conning silently, only his lips are moving.

It's the Bible again, because he wants to be good
And thinks somehow the book may tell him the secret.
He finds it raises more questions than it answers
And he has no intention of changing the way we live,
But he persists, the way some Catholics do.

The specs read, the teeth pronounce the story,
Chuckling, clacking, they may even be laughing.
Is this the book I ought to be writing, the one
For which they paid a good advance and gave
A deadline that passed two years ago?
If I could hear, I might take dictation.

Or, rather than the volume under contract,
Is it the story I always wanted to write,
About my 'other life', not the actual past
With its years of detour, its catalogue of blunder,
Those bankruptcies, those broken hearts (both ways),
But a past back-projected from a happy-ever-after,
Making fairy-tale sense, harvest-home piled high?

My lover who's young in the story is still around.
Without my specs I can't see, I feel his temperature.
I remember who he was, is that all written down? Look,
My specs gaze in his direction and my dentures
Smile at his warmth, and would be glad to kiss him
        If only they had lips.
I reach to touch him and the bedside light goes out.

The specs stop reading and abruptly sleep,
The teeth sigh, clamp shut, the book
Folds its hands in the dark across its stomach
And snores, the bed vibrates with it.
It's as if the bed is singing in short snatches,
A ballad maybe, or a hymn with its own illusions,
The celestial city, angels up and down
Like lift attendants in a grand hotel.

Ah, here he is, my lover, very warm beside me.
His darkness, his downed hard arm, his breathing.
The same for decades, still the space between us
In years is unchanged, though my eyes have debts,
My teeth depart like old folk from the parish,
And we still say we love each other to each other
And know what we mean, or think we know.
That's what the book under the lamp should be about.
I run my tongue over my pitted gums
I lick my lips as if I'm about to say something.

Annunciation

Cosimo de' Medici's Commission

Il Beato pinxit.
The deferential angel
    Won't leave her alone.
He comes from God and finds her
    In a bright loggia
Wistful, beautiful. He lands
    Armed with his lily,
A wand her presence magics
    Out of sight, a scent,
A spell her shy averted
Pallor, when she looks his way,
    Translates into prayer.

    This gorgeous angel's
Seen a thing or two: stood guard
    In Paradise, watched
The Serpent make sport of Eve,
    Published Adam's Fall;
Jerusalem he levelled,
    Towers, citizens,
Sweeping Israel's dust into
    The ugly mountain
We call Golgotha. He hears
Dull mallets drive the nails in.
    He tastes vinegar.

    Hail, he murmurs, *grace* ...
He who's God's sword, God's eagle,
    Earlier he's obeyed
Orders, soaring home on gold
    Untarnished pinions,

This time something's gone awry.
    She bends away, he
Wants her to attend, to touch.
    What is this, he says,
Can I become man? No, just
An angel, heavy haloed,
    Gold-winged, unable.

    Wretched Gabriel,
Who tend the orchard of souls,
    Plucking from night trees
The spirits we grow into,
    Who make prophets hear
Heaven's thunder in their hearts,
    Who give Zachary
The stupendous news of Christ,
    See her, attentive
To the message your lips say,
But to your gaze? Your honed wings –
    Dazzled by desire?

    Consider how she
Is just a girl, a pauper.
    And how old, angel,
You are: can you count up your
    Eternity? She
Could smell, if she desired to,
    How your gilded hair,
Handsome cheek, linen singlet
    Mulberry folds, hide
What would be ash if ever
You'd broken bread. You are not
    What she'd ever want.

About Homer: an epyllion

Ακόμα και ο Όμηρος νεύματα

Homer is old, he nods, at everything.
Tell me, O Muse, does he mean yes or no?
Perhaps he means *perhaps*. He nods agreeably.
    He sneezes
Into a red bandana the size of a bath-towel.

It's no surprise to see him. He tops the bill.
His presence has drawn the poets out.
Every single one wants to be like him –
    Well, not blind,
Not old, but immortal, name turned adjective.

He can still stand on his pair of ancient feet
In Birkenstocks (Arizona Regular), a grizzled
Statue roused from stone by archaeology and
    Adoration.
His jaw drops, he wails like an opera diva,

Spilling coloratura, then basso, bottomless.
The poets want to be like him. Not write like him.
Not write at all, in fact. Perform. They want
    Ovation,
Laurel crowns, tripods, money. How does he do it?

The audience eats out of his palm like a chicken pecking
Corn; all the applause and half the ticket sales
Are his, and he wins prizes despite his years.
    Dear Miles,
I wish you were sitting here, cross-legged, beside me.

You read him in Greek a long time ago at Wadham –
How would it be to come to the Singer of Tales
When you're old yourself? Lord and Parry were wrong,
    He's not a tradition.
He's skin and bone and a paunch, he needs a haircut;

You can smell him in the back row. Armpits. Onions.
He's senior to everyone else, even to Stanley
Who's got ten years on you, you've got ten on me:
    Go figure.
He's famously blind, too, as a bat, with, nowadays,

A yellow guide-dog and a white probing cane.
There was a time when a boy in scuffed chiton and sandals
Led him from gig to gig all over the classical world:
    Attica,
Boeotia, Corinth, Delphi, by boat to Lesbos, Mytilene,

Even Crete, and on the way home, Spartan Sparta.
Going from city to city they sometimes begged
A ride on a wagon, or Homer did, while the boy
    Cantered beside.
Hospitality was generally sparse; listeners

Listened out and cheered for their local heroes.
After a recital, those that could read and had money
Bought scrolls (one of the boy's jobs was to hump
    The scrollshop
From venue to venue on his little back

And ring up the drachmas). They'd get Homer to sign,
Steadying his twisted fingers on a biro.
When you think about it, the boy that guided him

       When Homer
First took to the road with poems and blank eye sockets

Can't have been immortal like the poet.
That first boy must have grown up and graduated,
Gone into farming or arts administration
       Or set out
To be a performer on his own, having heard the old man

Over and over and over, like a scratched record,
A very, very long scratch, retell the somber war
Of Greeks and Trojans, then, for light relief,
       The farce
Of that idiot Odysseus (the irony of the adjective 'wily'

Lost on audiences but never on his readers)
Stumbling and whoring the not very long
Way home to Ithaka, the tottering house,
       Penelope
No spring chicken, and taking a decade to get there;

Then as soon as he does and the dog wags its venerable tail
Slaying everything male that might be described as a suitor,
Apart from his son who's set out to seek him at every
       Bordello
And inn in the Ionian harbours and fortunately

Hasn't made it home yet, or he might have been for it
Along with the rest ... Homer's first guide-boy's successor,
Another bucolic brat, this time (for diversity) out of
       Parched Thessaly
Or further north, a Macedonian orphan, or an urchin

From Paeonia, will have earned crusts, kicks, an infrequent
Caress. – Nowadays dogs get a better deal than boys
Ever did, what with biscuits, chews and brushings,
    Regular vet care,
No one ever was cruel to a guide dog. Next summer

Homer's current Labrador will give way to a puppy
By the name of Waldo from outside Chesterfield.
– Being so old, Homer snoozes a lot of the time.
    Before recitals
He sits bolt upright on his stool and sleeps like a baby.

He doesn't look asleep, his sockets ajar.
If he held a paper cup folk would drop coins in,
Pat the dog and give him the time of day. He knows
    His poems
Off pat, or is it rather, that each time he pulls

The first line like a cork out of his heart,
The old old story wells up new as vintage ichor
And steaming? Though you know just where the story's
    Leading,
The words, always the same, carry a sense

Unique to the moment of utterance, you're charmed
Again, the wine dark sea is one time Thessalian
Limniona, the next a Moschofilero, or just plain
    Retsina;
The grey of Athene's eyes may be sea mist,

A churning dolphin, ash, whorled pearl or pumice.
He leads us on the story's single journey.
We bring, each of us, different luggage, and arrive

>   Uniquely
> Grieving, safe and sound, at Hector's ritual obsequies.

Being old myself, I've packed a thermos of brandy,
A knapsack with fruit and sandwiches, a rug,
Plus a change of clothes in case the poem's journey
>   Extends
Beyond the advertised time and the last train home.

My mobile is fully charged so I can take photos.
His recitals vary a lot though the words spoken
Are the same each night. The torches cast different shadows.
>   Whatever
Homer sees is outline. We fill in dimension and hue.

The poem latches on to each listener: it keeps me
Watching the dog who's delivered the poet on stage
And sits like Patience by his side, not listening but lolling
>   Its tongue,
Then gnawing at an itch low down by its pink boner.

Eventually the dog subsides, puts its chin on its paws.
It starts snoring gently, gently. Its legs twitch.
Homer marches us on, into battle again.
>   Swords drawn,
We hack at the waves, we rush the wine dark tide.

Tell me, O Muse, will the story ever be over?